COTTAGE STYLE
A Palette of White

COTTAGE STYLE

A Palette of White

FROM THE PUBLISHERS OF

the **cottage**® *journal* MAGAZINE

COTTAGE STYLE
A Palette of White

PRESIDENT Phyllis Hoffman DePiano
EXECUTIVE VICE PRESIDENT/CCO Brian Hart Hoffman
VICE PRESIDENT/EDITORIAL Cindy Smith Cooper
ART DIRECTOR Jodi Rankin Daniels

EDITORIAL
EDITOR Linda Baltzell Wright
CREATIVE DIRECTOR/PHOTOGRAPHY Mac Jamieson
ASSOCIATE EDITOR Katie Wood
EDITORIAL ASSISTANT Kellie Grammer
COPY EDITOR Whitney Law
CONTRIBUTING WRITERS
Karen Callaway, Alice Welsh Doyle, Lauren Eberle, Lisa Frederick,
Vicki Ingham, Robert C. Martin, Faith Morgan, Ann Zimmerman
CONTRIBUTING STYLIST Yukie McLean
SENIOR PHOTOGRAPHERS John O'Hagan, Marcy Black Simpson
PHOTOGRAPHERS
Jim Bathie, William Dickey, Stephanie Welbourne
CONTRIBUTING PHOTOGRAPHERS
Colleen Duffley, Lauren Rubinstein, Scot Zimmerman
SENIOR DIGITAL IMAGING SPECIALIST Delisa McDaniel
DIGITAL IMAGING SPECIALIST Clark Densmore

DIGITAL MEDIA
MULTIMEDIA DIRECTOR Bart Clayton
ONLINE EDITOR Victoria Phillips
VIDEOGRAPHER Aaron Spigner
DIGITAL GRAPHIC DESIGNER Alana Hogg

CONSUMER MARKETING
CONSUMER MARKETING DIRECTOR Tricia Wagner Williams

ADMINISTRATIVE
HUMAN RESOURCES DIRECTOR Judy Brown Lazenby
IT DIRECTOR Matthew Scott Holt
DEALER PROGRAM MANAGER Janice Ritter
PRODUCTION ASSISTANT Rachel Collins

Front cover photography by Colleen Duffley.

hm | books

PRESIDENT Phyllis Hoffman DePiano
EXECUTIVE VICE PRESIDENT/COO Eric W. Hoffman
EXECUTIVE VICE PRESIDENT/CCO Brian Hart Hoffman
VICE PRESIDENT/DIGITAL MEDIA Jon Adamson
VICE PRESIDENT/MANUFACTURING Greg Baugh
VICE PRESIDENT/EDITORIAL Cindy Smith Cooper
VICE PRESIDENT/ADMINISTRATION Lynn Lee Terry

Sign up for *The Cottage Journal's* newsletter at *thecottagejournal.com*.

EDITORIAL & ADVERTISING SALES OFFICES
1900 International Park Drive, Suite 50, Birmingham, AL 35243
Phone: 205-995-8860, 888-411-8995   Fax: 205-380-2740
Website: *thecottagejournal.com*

CUSTOMER SERVICE
The Cottage Journal, P.O. Box 6201, Harlan, IA 51593
Phone: 888-393-6246   E-mail: CJScustserv@cdsfulfillment.com

Hoffman Media
1900 International Park Drive, Suite 50
Birmingham, Alabama 35243
www.hoffmanmedia.com

ISBN # 978-1-940772-17-2

CONTENTS

INTRODUCTION

Cottage style has long incited idyllic visions of effortless charm and timeworn elegance. It is this enchanting reflection that makes this aesthetic not only a favorite decorating scheme but also a romantic frame of mind. It's a style that enables us to combine precious heirloom pieces with bold accents teaming with personality to weave together a story of home, heart, and history.

This book explores light-filled rooms cloaked in shades of white and neutrals that create beautiful, personal spaces. When layered with inviting textures, interesting finishes, varying hues, and a combination of modern details, you'll find that decorating with white creates both a calming retreat and a lasting space that feels both cozy and chic.

No matter the style of your home, an interior palette of white lends an ethereal air of timeless tranquility and spaciousness. This stunning collection of cottages compiled from the pages of *The Cottage Journal* magazine offers inspired style ideas for your home that cherish the ordinary, embrace imperfections, celebrate treasured heirlooms, and welcome you home in a fresh, new way.

CHAPTER ONE

COTTAGE STYLE INSPIRATION

OPEN &
AIRY

A white house is like a crisp white shirt—it's
timeless and never goes out of style.

The Sandquists' charming cottage sits on 6 acres of beach property that is mostly covered in wild palmetto bushes. That's how Sherry Sandquist came up with the name Palmetto Cottage for both their home and her business. "I've owned an antiques and interiors business for the last 20 years and sell items similar to items I use to decorate my own home," she says. Junk stores and antiques shops are Sherry's favorite haunts for finding furnishings.

"I've always loved white rooms. They lift my spirit just being in them," she explains. "White opens up all possibilities in decorating, allowing me to totally change the feel of a room just by changing out pillows, art, or accessories." Nearly four years ago Sherry took the plunge and painted their floors a high-gloss white from Benjamin Moore. Sherry says the result was surprisingly easy to clean and really opened up the house. The walls were already painted "Decorator's White" from Benjamin Moore.

When asked about her favorite thing about their cottage, she says, "It's the open airiness. We've lived with white surroundings for the past 25 years, and I still have no desire to experiment with any other color." ⒸⓈ

Sherry's father made quite a few pieces of furniture, including the daybed seen here in the living room. The round corner table was pulled from her parents' backyard after weathering there for about 10 years.

Grays is one of Sherry's favorite colors for home accents, as seen in the bedroom's linens and upholstery.

COASTAL BEACH COTTAGE

At Manasquan, New Jersey, beach lovers adore sunning on the broad sandy beach, surfing the inlet, fishing the river and ocean, boating, and catching a bite at the friendly local eateries. This beach cottage celebrates happy summer days at the Jersey Shore.

The beach is only a two–minute walk from the front door, and the décor carries the shore experience inside with collected beach glass, a salvaged ship's porthole, and the sunny yellow paint against the cheerful white woodwork.

*V*acation cottages demand a relaxed simplicity. Through its colors and informality, this one does just that while providing a sense of place. The local Manasquan team at Imagineered Homes, LLC, designed, built, selected the colors, and furnished the home driven by a vision of joyous leisure.

The painted woodwork and furniture follow the tradition of vacation cottages. The attractive perforated cabinet-front screen hides the television and enhances a sense of getting away from it all.

The landing (above) features an innovative display of family snapshots using a mock beach fence made from weathered wood and wire. Resting below and retired from use are a lifeguard's rescue swim board and a pair of worn oars.

In the bedroom, the shell pink of the side table and linens and the authentically nautical lamp combine with the artwork of a surfer perfectly catching a wave to make it difficult to sleep away the day and miss the fun to be had at the shore. ⚞

CHANGING SPACES

This traditional family home gets a fresh makeover by opening up spaces for entertaining.

Before this homeowner began rennovations the kitchen had a small door that completely isolated the cook from the guests in the great room. The door and wall were removed to open the space between the two rooms, creating easy traffic flow and an airy feel.

ometimes a change of season has less to do with the weather and more to do with the season of our lives. This was exactly the case with homeowner Rosa Hooper and her kitchen renovation.

With the graduation of her youngest son quickly approaching, Rosa was about to be an empty nester, and she felt it was the perfect time to make some changes in her home that she had put off. With the help of designer Mandi Smith T, she was able to make her home more suitable for her needs. By selecting materials and furnishings that play between modern and rustic, Rosa was able to achieve a casual and updated environment. From a small evening at home cooking with friends to hosting a full afternoon of football for a crowd, the spaces now do double duty. CS

STYLE IDEA For a casual yet clean appearance within glass-front cabinets, stick to one color for all dishware and serving pieces. This will keep the cabinets looking fresh and stylish.

CLASSIC LIVING

Narnia is not only a classic when it comes to children's literature; it's also a revered beach house found along Florida's Gulf Coast.

esigning a beach house that combines the quaintness of a coastal retreat with the sophistication of a New York townhome is no easy feat, but when executed by renowned architectural firm Robert A. M. Stern, it becomes a project to emulate. As if the task weren't daunting enough, Stern, along with design partner Gary Brewer, added elements of 1930s Swedish classicism to this beautifully articulated home located in Seaside, Florida.

Shipshape Space

Since every square inch of this beach house is designed as prudently as a ship's cabin, the best choice for cooking space was a galley kitchen.

STYLE IDEA As with many beach houses, there are often more guests than beds, and space is at a premium. To remedy this, a sleeping nook was built into the room much like a window seat found in older homes. Also, a handy trundle bed that's cleverly concealed by the

(Right) In keeping with the architecture's nod to Swedish classicism, the furniture and accessories in Narnia evoke a traditional, restrained elegance.

(Below) This storybook home comes to life through an amalgam of architectural styles. The ground floor resembles a stone base but is actually made entirely of wood.

(Opposite) A collection of colorful shells placed on a mirror–topped dresser is an obvious yet effective way to accessorize with the beach's natural treasures. (Above) A balanced alcove of windows and tucked–in shelves creates a cozy retreat for the master bed.

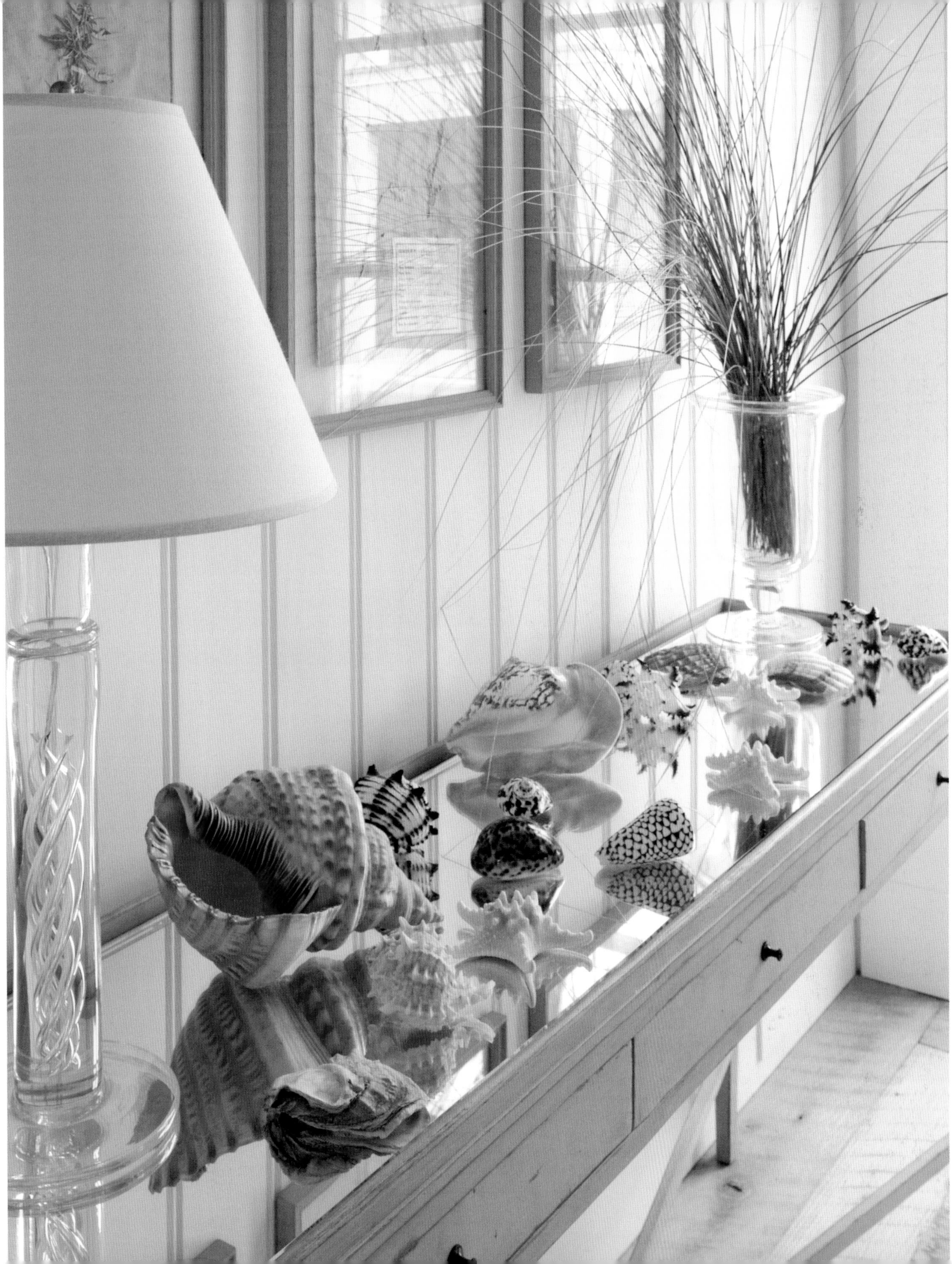

TRANQUIL DELIGHT

Developed from a harmonious vision, this South Carolina cottage offers a breezy retreat from the everyday.

The designer and the homeowners were in agreement: They wanted to create a vacation home that spoke to a classic coastal sensibility without interpreting the theme too literally. They didn't want to be too heavy-handed, notes interior designer Grace Cribbin, adding that they steered clear of the standard use of shells and nautical accents to reference the home's Kiawah Island setting.

One of the most important elements driving the home's interior design was the abundance of windows. The light-filled rooms with sweeping views of the adjoining golf course influenced the decisions of using few window treatments so as not to compete with the view.

"Using cabinetry designed with freestanding legs gave
a more open, classic feel in the dining room and kitchen."

Grace Cribbin

A mosaic backsplash is
the centerpiece of this
kitchen design, while
the draperies echo the
two-tone paint colors.

Relaxed Elegance

The homeowners wanted a sense of serenity and sophisticated relaxation in their vacation home. Everything was to be understated—nothing fussy or overdone. Grace's use of a tranquil, neutral white palette in the master bedroom is made more interesting by the subtle patterns of the linens. Soft stripes, damask, and coral motifs work together in these low-contrast coordinating colors.

The airy and soft white color palette was inspired by the tranquil surroundings that the homeowners treasured. A close proximity to the beach yielded the calming coastal color scheme. Seaside elements such as water, sand, and coral informed the hues throughout the home, but the inspiration is most prominently displayed in the bedrooms where the calming sense of an ocean escape is relaxing and soothing.

Grace also steered the couple to choose neutral materials for the larger furniture items in their home, including the sofas and upholstered headboards. That way, color is introduced through pillows and other small accessories, which can be changed out seasonally or as the couple's taste changes.

Whether used for weekend escapes or extended vacations, this cottage getaway has become a calm respite indicative of its natural surroundings and the rapport between homeowners and designer. GS

STYLE INSPIRATIONS

Cottage style evokes a romantic elegance and timeworn charm as it blends antique elements with modern details. Decorating with soft white ruffles, painted furniture, treasured collections, and personal pieces that tell a story is an easy way to incorporate cottage style into your home.

Don't hide your hobby in a closet if it is something that can artfully be incorporated into your living space.

CHAPTER TWO

WHITE SUN-FILLED ROOMS

NATURAL BEAUTY

A Georgia designer proves that family–friendly comfort needn't sacrifice style.

ikie Barfield had dreams of pursuing interior design. But life—and a law degree—guided the accomplished attorney on a different path. She and her husband fell for their darling 1920s cottage in Decatur, Georgia. "The Tudor windows won me over," Nikie recalls. "We couldn't resist the home's charm, even though we knew we'd have a lot of work ahead of us."

As it turns out the renovation was just the spark it took to reignite Nikie's previous passion. "I fell back in love with the whole design process—the creativity, the textures, the fabrics, the styling."

Rather than another piece of wall art, this statuesque Swedish Mora clock was chosen for its architectural interest.

Her style is classic and natural; she chooses timeless, neutral backdrops and infuses a hint of color and a nod to nature. Take, for instance, the kitchen, where a weathered table and farmhouse sink balance crisp white marble countertops and stainless appliances. "The mix of Old World and New World takes the edge off contemporary style and makes any space appear more approachable," Nikie explains. Well-curated accessories such as glass globe bottles and an antique scale add interest, while a simple light blue background makes the white, glass-front cabinets pop.

In the living room, a contemporary animal rug anchors an antique European coffee table, stone mantel, and structured chairs. "Hide is one of my favorite family-friendly rugs, since it's natural, budget-friendly, and durable for children," Nikie shares.

STYLE IDEA Maximize the impact of a small, sun-splashed space with light linens and paint. Then, guide the eye upward with soaring bedposts and a striking chandelier.

"I fell back in love with the whole design process—the creativity, the textures, the fabrics, the styling."

Nikie Barfield

Upstairs, a formerly unusable attic was transformed into a sunny master suite with steeply pitched ceilings and a spa-like bathroom. "My favorite part of this space is the antique dressing table," Nikie says. "Its classic patina balances the crisp, white beadboard and breathes new life into the whole room."

Throughout the home, bowls, vases, and even antique crocks cradle apples, tulips, ferns, and other houseplants. "Styling is a big part of the design package. Fruit and flowers go a long way in establishing an inviting feel. They're easy to change out with the season, plus they add so much pleasure," Nikie says. "Often we're so busy that we forget to enjoy our surroundings. But, simply put, our homes are made to enjoy."

A Swedish apothecary cabinet takes a standard mudroom from functional to fantastic. Each family member has a row designated for stylish shoe storage with room to spare for day-to-day necessities.

AN ORGANIZED PLAN

Crab Point guest cottage takes a page from classic beach dwellings of the early 1900s with historic details and rooms designed to take full advantage of the island views.

What do you need to create the ideal guest cottage experience? Try a pristine setting with beautiful views and a home that is both lovely and functional to satisfy even the pickiest of visitors. Joanne and Bruce Montgomery had an enviable location to work with on Whidbey Island in the Puget Sound, about 25 miles north of Seattle. They also had the good sense to engage Ross Chapin, a local architect who specializes in small space design.

"We wanted Crab Point to feel like a classic beach cottage from the 1910s," Bruce says. "We included an extensive use of wood walls, wainscoting, and details in the carpentry to create a historic look." The petite cottage is only 1,200 square feet but feels more spacious due to the floor plan and clever use of built-ins. "Storage should not be forgotten, especially in a small house, where clutter can quickly overwhelm," Ross says. "Built-in cabinets and shelves are a terrific means for taming the storage issue in an elegant way." Another space-saving design element is a built-in eating alcove, which has a smaller footprint than a traditional dining room table and chairs.

A custom built-in dining nook saves space and provides an intimate place for meals. The blue-and-white cushions play into the subtle nautical theme of the cottage.

The great room with high ceilings is the heart of the home with its abundance of windows that flood the space with light and views.

Beadboard walls bring vintage character to an airy white living space.

(Below) The 1,200-square-foot guesthouse uses custom built-ins to maximize space and keep clutter contained.

With the impressive views (the house is set on a point), lush gardens, and a pretty front porch, the interiors could have been an afterthought, but instead, they bring a connectedness that makes the rooms flow with comfort and ease. A classic blue-and-white palette with striped and printed fabrics, light wood floors, white walls, and nautical accents showcases that classic beach cabin style the Montgomerys wanted to replicate, but there is also practical in the pretty. "The wood floors are hickory, which has a very knotty look but is one of the hardest hard woods and holds up well given all the sand that can be tracked through the house," Joanne notes. With everything about the cottage so meticulously planned, there is no doubt that every guest will long for a return invitation to Crab Point. ⌂

HOME
WITH
HEART

Despite its tiny footprint, this garden–inspired
California cottage lives large.

The first time Julie and Brian O'Keefe walked into their 1950s cottage in the hills above Los Angeles, Julie was ready to walk right back out. "It had absolutely zero character," she says. Its 1,300 square feet were a mishmash of dated surfaces, bland architecture, and an uninspired layout. But Brian, who saw potential beneath its plainness, persuaded Julie to put her design eye to work.

"He had the vision, and I executed it," Julie says.

In the kitchen, a vintage bowl corrals fresh basil, thyme, and parsley, which Julie uses for cooking before it's planted in the herb garden outside. And she repurposed a vintage baguette bin to hold kitchen trash.

HERBS
les herbs
SAGE
la sauge
MINT
la menthe
TARRAGON
l'estragon
ANISE
l'anis
CHERVIL
le cerfeuil
LAVENDER
la lavande
BASIL
le basilic
MARJORAM

PURE BUTTER

Changing the floor plan wasn't in the cards, so the couple focused on freshening the home's face. Hickory flooring went down; tongue-and-groove ceilings went up. Julie cloaked the walls, ceilings, and cabinetry in a fresh palette of white for a sense of openness and flow, as well as a neutral backdrop on which to accent different plants and accessories each season. An old lava-rock hearth was replaced with one made of stone, and Brian recently added a greenhouse.

Julie, who owned the Los Angeles-area shop Julie O'Keefe Home and Garden for nearly 20 years, infused their home with lived-in cottage style: natural, creamy white fabrics and faded florals, textural woods and vintage finds. Given the limited space, every piece of furniture needed to pull its weight. The O'Keefes chose antique case goods that would double as storage for treasured collections, such as quilts, white ironstone, antique garden tools, and more.

The master bedroom's red–and–white palette came from the red bottlebrush and white hibiscus that bloom outside the windows. Pillows made from gently worn linens set off the vintage quilt.

Perhaps nothing informs the décor more strongly than Julie's love for gardening, which she inherited from her mother. "It just adds such warmth," Julie says. Southern California weather lends itself to indoor-outdoor living, and the lush plantings around the house bring a touch of the garden in through the open doors. Julie planted tumbles of old-fashioned flowers that would have staying power long after she cut them to bring indoors, including daffodils, sweet peas, and roses.

That sense of familiarity is what lies behind the home's charm. "It's very casual and warm and friendly and cozy and approachable," Julie says. "I wanted people to feel comfortable." ⊂S

(Left) A vintage English garden tool holds back the sheer curtain panels that frame the doorway, looking out to the garden. (Right) The deck is the O'Keefes' favorite place to enjoy the outdoors. "We entertain there whenever we can," Julie says. "It's an extension of our living space."

SEASIDE SERENITY

The famous white sands of a gulf-coast community provide inspiration for the look and color palette of this waterfront retreat that's beachy fun for the whole family.

This Seaside, Florida, rental proves that crisp and white can still be family-friendly. While something so neutral might traditionally be associated with a sleek and modern design, cozy furnishings and playful accents give this cottage a more casual and home-like feeling. Texture and slight tonal variations add interest to this mostly white color palette. In the kitchen a tabby fireplace surround and white marble countertops season the space with lasting style. Natural rugs soften the hardwood floors while stainless and chrome fixtures sparkle in the sunlight that streams through the windows. A few coastal-inspired pops of color in the form of cheery pillows, ceramic accents, and rainbow-hued artwork are scattered around the space. CS

Sea Clearly

With its open floor plan and abundance of windows, there's no shortage of ways to enjoy the brilliant panoramic beach view from this cottage home—whether it's curling up with a favorite book in a comfy chair or enjoying a friendly chat over your morning cup of coffee at the game table.

Cozy pillows and simple florals serve as the only colorful accents in this all-white space, while maple hardwood floors provide the perfect backdrop for a natural, sea grass rug.

ROOM TO RELAX

Get inspired by this beach guest cottage, and turn your own home into a whitewashed mini-escape. Whether you live by the seaside or you're totally land-locked, this tranquil color scheme is simply delightful.

Abundant natural light bounces off the semi-gloss finish of the painted wood walls and ceiling lending an airy glow to the entire space. Cozier textures like cotton and linen balance the sleek painted surroundings.

esigned by acclaimed architect Scott Merrill, this sweet Seaside, Florida, rental mimics some of the features of Thomas Jefferson's own honeymoon cottage on the grounds of Monticello. But instead of a presidential look, this getaway was built with beachy romance in mind. All white walls, dressings, and furnishings set a peaceful and quiet tone for the space. An abundant porch area takes advantage of the calming sea breeze allowing guests to relax as they doze in the hammock or take advantage of the screen porch Jacuzzi. The wealth of windows are perfect for enjoying the sea views and salty air while relaxing indoors.

CREATIVE DESIGN

An affinity for design and an eye for balance combine to create a bright, inspiring, and comfortable family home.

A beautiful home is essential to Laura Clark's creative process. As an artist, she relies on her painting techniques—starting with a basic composition and building upon it—to craft the ideal space for her young family. "Good design both reflects and encourages creativity," Laura says. "Achieving a beautiful design is a challenge that excites me—searching for and finding the right pieces to complete the overall composition in a way that feels balanced and whole and still true to my personality."

Refreshing whites and calm neutral tones serve as her canvas as Laura uses layers of upholstered pieces, sleek silhouettes, ornate details, and modern touches to create the perfect juxtaposition. She leaves windows unobstructed by heavy drapes and utilizes mirrors to reflect natural light around the room, adding to the airy feel of the space.

Laura has worked to create a home that is both inspired by and inspiring for her creative work, and through her thoughtful design she has achieved just that. ⌘

A few playful elements are an asset in this well-designed space. Child-sized Louis Ghost chairs are arranged near an antique loveseat for a whimsical, light-hearted look.

Laura adds visual interest with unique light fixtures and carefully chosen accessories. She loves the impact a large, sculptural chandelier can have on the atmosphere of a room.

"Good design both reflects and encourages creativity."

Laura Clark

STYLE INSPIRATIONS

The secret to keeping light-filled rooms feeling open and airy is using soft, delicate bed linens and ethereal, translucent curtains that allow light to pour through without becoming too heavy.

CHAPTER THREE

SHADES OF WHITE

A STORIED COTTAGE

Once home to artists Georges and Eleanor Bridges, this 1921 studio cottage influenced by Greek and Spanish architecture is now drenched in a palette of white. Despite the fresh paint, the new owners allow the home's vibrant history to shine through.

iana and Eric Hansen are only the second owners of this unique cottage. "It had been empty for about three years before we bought it," Diana says. "I had been in the house 12 years earlier, and Eleanor showed me around and pointed out the pieces Georges had made. I never dreamed then that I would be living in the house one day."

The cottage boasts a rich history of well-known guests. Aviation pioneer Amelia Earhart was a school roommate of Eleanor's who visited the home, and when Georges and Eleanor studied art in Europe they befriended authors Ernest Hemingway and F. Scott Fitzgerald who also visited the cottage on occasion.

Designed in 1921 as a studio, the ceiling of the main room was 26 feet high to accommodate Eleanor's large paintings and Georges's sculptures. Diana said Georges and Eleanor eventually added a balcony so they could include two bedrooms upstairs, which was about the same time they built the kitchen. "The kitchen is exactly the same today. Eleanor hosted huge parties from this little bitty kitchen," she explains.

Diana's love of all things white can also be seen in her popular gift shop, White Flowers.

"When we rented the piano
for a garden wedding party
the man painted it white
for us. It looked so beautiful
we decided to buy it even
though we don't play."

Diana Hansen

The home was originally very colorful, painted in mustard, turquoise, and other popular colors of the 1920s. "When we moved in, first thing we did was paint everything white," Diana says. "Now you can see the beautiful designs and details." Georges and Eleanor enjoyed their studio and home for 69 years. The Hansens have called it home for 30 years and hope to enjoy it for at least 30 more. ❧

Georges sculpted the metal mantel and attached what looks like metal trivets or plates for added detail. He also created the andirons. The original fireside bench is decorated with Eleanor's needlework.

Georges built the studio's doors and even forged the hardware. The table and bench are original to the home but were a dark wood until Diana painted them white.

SIMPLY SERENE

If beauty comes in small packages, then this cottage fits the description.
Soft shades of cream give an open, spacious feel to the space.

A chance to create a stylish setting that is filled with texture and yet calming to its owner proved to be the task at hand for Pandy Agnew, the decorator of this cozy cottage. From the chandelier in the dining area with all of its rustic roping details to the rattan-backed breakfast chairs, the eye is entertained. The elements of surprise are having wall sconces, a narrower dining table, and strategically placing mirrors to make the small space seem larger and reflect light throughout. Varying tones of wood also add to the quaint interior design. Purposely without floor rugs, the warm wood shines while giving the entire cottage an open and welcoming sense of home.

"We pushed the 'refresh' button and lightened up the space as we took off a couple of decades with this interior."

Pandy Agnew

Reflections of Light

A distressed milk paint finish was added to this glass–paned armoire that sits in the entry. The background was painted white to show off collectibles.

FOCUS ON WHITE

This timeless family cottage incorporates Louisiana–inspired accents to its monochromatic scheme, adding a personal flavor that still feels polished.

To keep the crisp white interiors of the home from being too monochromatic, the owners gravitated toward fabrics and patterns in light creams, grays, and muted blues. This color combination sets a soothing, comfortable tone in the living area and throughout the house.

With the kitchen, breakfast, and living areas combined into one space, this open plan proves ideal for both entertaining and daily living. Adjoining the kitchen and living area, the breakfast and casual dining nook contains a series of casement windows, which serves as the primary source of natural light for the space. Polished marble called Calcutta Gold White was used for their countertops, which complement the stainless-steel appliances and white subway tile backsplash.

Conveniently tucked in between the kitchen and dining room, the butler's pantry enables the main cooking space to stay less cluttered and chaotic. The cabinets have a more casual, cottage look, which is mirrored by the white apron-front sink and natural butcher-block countertops.

STYLE IDEA Using the same paint color but in a different finish varies the look of the paint. This opening is painted in a high-gloss version of Conservative Gray from Sherwin-Williams. The moldings in the room are also painted in high gloss, but the walls have an eggshell finish in the same color.

Built underneath the stairway leading to the second floor, a wine storage cabinet contains enough space for 200 bottles. It's located directly across the hall from the formal dining room and right around the corner from the kitchen.

The deep cased opening leading into the formal dining room from the hall was designed to set the room apart. Rather than being just another entry, the panels give the dining room a sense of formality not found in the rest of the house. An alcove in the dining room adorned with artwork depicting Louisiana pelicans serves as an ideal spot for a bar caddy.

The master bedroom appropriately contains some of the owners' favorite finds, such as an intricately woven rug, matching side tables, and bayou-themed artwork. The antique gold finish of the tables, paired with neutral linens and white walls, creates a tranquil spot for rest and relaxation. CS

To really jazz up their master bath and vanity areas, the owners cleverly took 12-inch square Carrera white marble tiles, cut them in half, and then laid them in a herringbone pattern. This method is a great way to add character to a standard-sized tile.

The master closet is a picture of organization and more importantly, equal space. A central dressing island from Wellborn Cabinet, Inc. is outfitted with shoe racks on both sides, which makes finding shoes an easy task.

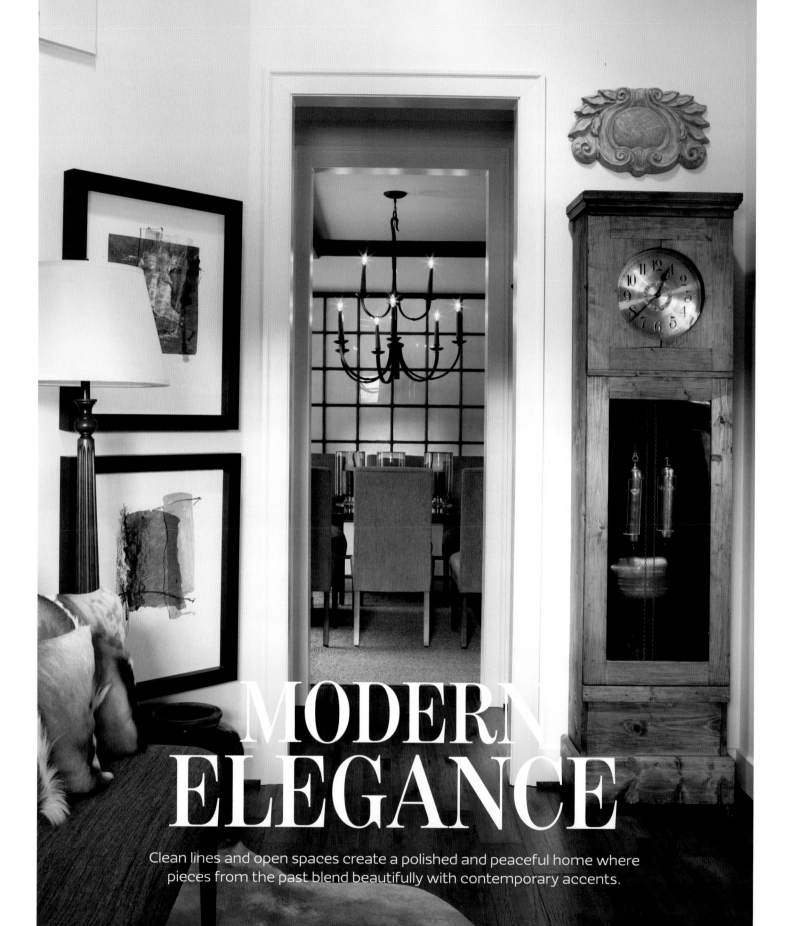

MODERN ELEGANCE

Clean lines and open spaces create a polished and peaceful home where pieces from the past blend beautifully with contemporary accents.

The first accessory chosen for the living room was the painting by Scott's mother that hangs over the mantel. He already owned all of the major upholstered pieces, which were classic in style, then brought in modern touches with a mirrored-glass coffee table and geometric-print chairs (as seen on page 121.)

andscape designer Scott Gilchrist is just as adept at creating beautiful home interiors as he is at designing dazzling English perennial gardens. Though his indoor décor boasts a decidedly more subdued palette than the hollyhocks and delphiniums growing in the garden, it is anything but vanilla.

Scott worked with noted architect Jim Barganier to make a few tweaks to the builder's spec-home blueprint. With this, his fifth house, Scott has honed and refined his personal style, resulting in a residence that is the perfect mix of formal and casual, old and new, straight lines and elegant curves—and suits the self-professed "neat freak" to a tee.

The home's eclectic composition shines as soon as the front door opens. In the foyer, modern artwork from Sante Fe, New Mexico, hangs alongside an antique grandfather clock refurbished by Scott's late father. A multi-paned window covers one wall of the dining room—a serendipitous find that, in a delightfully surprising twist, turned out to be from his grandmother's old house. With panes now glazed in silver metallic paint, it is both a striking and sentimental piece of art.

Each room employs a restrained use of color that enhances the neutral scheme. And the white palatte, along with the juxtaposition of contemporary and classic furnishings, creates the restful surroundings the accomplished designer is happy to call home. CS

"While I can appreciate the new trend for more colorful interiors, I prefer mostly neutral for my own."

Scott Gilchrist

"I live pretty casually, and I have the dishes I use on a regular basis close at hand," Scott says. It keeps the dining room from looking too formal."

STYLE IDEA When working with a small space, the decorator suggested finding furniture pieces that could be utilized in more than one way, like the side tables pictured here that can also be used as stools for extra seating in the kitchen or living area.

SMALL & SIMPLE

This tiny Katrina cottage has just enough space for simple seaside living.

When people visit Brenda Speller's tiny Katrina cottage, their lasting impression tends to be a sentiment of "this is all you really need in life." Though her one-bedroom cottage provides less than 600 square feet of living space, it offers a simplistic solution to beach living.

Brenda decided to move to the beach after retiring from 20 years of service in the military. The undeveloped wooded property she owned in Seacrest, Florida, housed two small buildings, a washroom and a one-room guest bungalow, and allowed just enough space to add a prefabricated Katrina cottage. Brenda gutted the cottage to create a simple home that maximized every inch. And with the help of interior decorator Tonya G. Kilpatrick she was able to employ a few design tricks to make the space feel larger.

When she remodeled the kitchen Brenda knew she needed to get rid of the big overhead cabinets and large furnishings. She scaled down all of her appliances, opting for an under the counter refrigerator and a small stove-top oven. She installed wall racks for shelving and found a 20-inch-square butcher-block island from Ikea. "We got small furniture so the house wouldn't look so small," Brenda shares, noting she specifically selected other things like a light granite countertop, white paint for the walls, and bamboo flooring all to create a more open look. ⟨S⟩

"Creating a real modern-looking kitchen in that small space and being able to give that area a 'wow factor' was so much fun!"

Tonya G. Kilpatrick

Although working with a small budget, Tonya pulled together a luxe look in Brenda's bedroom by crafting a headboard from plywood, batting, and fabric. "If we saw something we liked, we figured out how to do it," Brenda says.

BLEND OF
OLD AND NEW

A family of five blends comfort and style in this charming cottage that easily mixes cherished heirloom furnishings with fun, new finds.

Homeowners Will and Kathryn McCraney knew they loved their 1921 Mississippi cottage before they even moved in. "When we were still in graduate school, I walked by the house and told the people who lived there, 'If you ever sell your house call me,'" Kathryn says. "They called two days later!" The McCraneys have since created an inviting home whose charming curb appeal is carried throughout the cottage's interior. Layered in a crisp palette of white, the McCraney home offers a family-friendly environment by pulling in cherished heirlooms and handmade pieces that add loads of warmth and a personal touch. "I think if you love your house you can put your personality into it, and my personality is a little bit old and a little bit new," Kathryn says.

The square-shaped dining room made opting for a round table a simple choice. The neutral space feels fresh, taking color cues from the Oushak rug and artwork by local artist Stacy Underwood. "None of it was necessarily meant to go together," Kathryn shares. "It just kind of all works together."

Bold Pop of Color

Decorator Lynn Myers encouraged Kathryn to add the vibrant lime green banquette to her sleek, white kitchen. Without that encouragement, Kathryn says she probably would have gone for an all-white space, but with a family of five and lots of pets, the McCraneys needed the high-traffic area to be both functional and forgiving of everyday messes. The breakfast nook is accented with acrylic chairs and framed bird prints that were a Christmas gift from her husband, Will.

The McCraneys' home appears to effortlessly blend new, modern pieces with family antiques. And that traditional style mirrors the essence of their home. When a decorator helped them renovate nearly 15 years ago, it was important for them to stay true to the character of the cottage while adding some modern amenities. "The best help you can get is someone who doesn't tell you to buy everything new and just start over," Kathryn says. "Some things certainly need to be retired, but I think a good decorator will help you incorporate what you already have, rather than tell you everything needs to be new." ⬛

In the master bedroom Kathryn opted for an accent wall of wallpaper. "I feel like you get a lot of bang for your buck to do the wallpaper versus a piece of artwork," she says of her bedroom's focal point. "I love the cleanness of the white and the gold." The on-suite master bath is drenched in a palette of creamy whites that with the help of the room's natural light create a tranquil setting that feels larger than it is.

CONTEMPORARY COTTAGE

With the help of a designer, this young homeowner creates a comfortable style that effortlessly blends natural elements with sophisticated glamour.

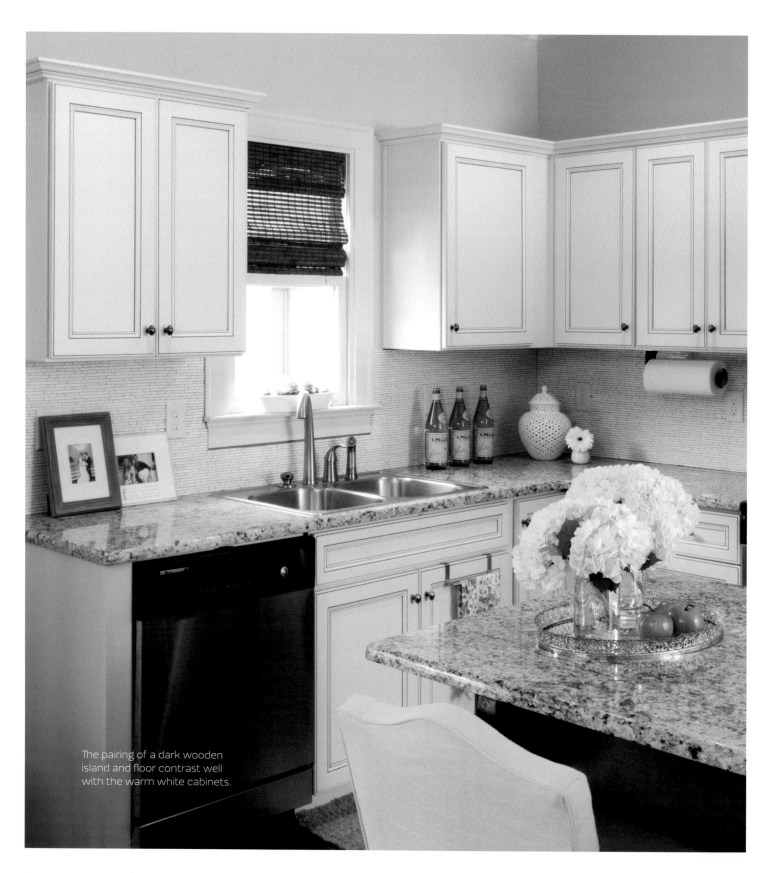

The pairing of a dark wooden island and floor contrast well with the warm white cabinets.

Homeowner Kelli Burton says that before she met her interior designer and friend, Laurel-Dawn McBurney, she was unsure of her personal design style. But after being guided by Laurel-Dawn's expert knowledge, Kelli has since found her true style—a style she describes as "rustic glamour." "I love bringing outside textures inside," Kelli says, adding they used driftwood accents and natural wood furnishings to balance the sheen of her decorative elements.

Warm brown walls and flooring in the living room add a dramatic backdrop to the white sofa and whitewashed curio.

A tone-on-tone painted headboard adds a playful look in the guest bedroom.

A neutral color palette, punctuated by a smattering of warm yellows and cool greens, highlights the interesting textures of the materials used in the home and allows them to take center stage. The comfortable, collected feel of Kelli's accessories and furnishings lends an interesting patina to what could have been simply a neutral new home.

From the light fixtures to the decorative accessories, a plethora of metallic accents sparkle throughout. "Laurel-Dawn always told me to use both gold and silver together, that it adds glamour to the space," Kelli says.

Beyond aesthetics, the cottage's living spaces and furniture layout have been customized to suit Kelli and her husband's lifestyle. Their penchant for entertaining is made easier by an airy, open floor plan. "You can be in the kitchen cooking but still be able to socialize with guests that are in the den," she says. More importantly, the design is compatible with the couple's day-to-day activities. "We wanted practical and comfortable; we wanted to be able to really live in the space," Kelli says, which is exactly what they accomplished.

STYLE INSPIRATIONS

Decorating with shades of white is all about layering textures. Whitewashed walls feel softer when accented with linen slipcovers lined with ruffles. And a white room can become more visually interesting when decorating with architectural elements like white, weatherworn shutters or columns.

CHAPTER FOUR

ACCESSORIZING A WHITE PALETTE

FRESH NEW STYLE

A mother of three upgrades her home's basic tone-on-tone style for an infusion of monochromatic pattern and personality.

ecorating a home in soft monochromatic shades of cream and white doesn't have to translate to a plain or simple space void of color and character. Homeowner Louise Plott knows that the key to decorating with neutrals is all about layering and incorporating different textures and interesting, unexpected color accents. With this in mind, Louise created an inviting home that while neutral in palatte is rich in personal charms. "My designer will be the first to tell you that I know what I like. I'm not afraid of fun and funky," Louise shares.

The homeowner had her builder open this previously walled-off staircase and install stunning ironwork.

In the living room, Louise and designer Lisa Flake of Caldwell Flake Interiors steered clear of "stuffy" and opted for comfortable sitting areas, graphic window treatments, a brilliant sunburst, and large, sentimental paintings created by local artists all while maintaining an understated creamy white base. Throughout the room, sizeable drum shades from a local lighting fixtures and antiques shop add interesting scale.

And in Louise's home, she makes sure that her monochromatic furnishings are not only comfortable but also kid-friendly. "Perhaps my favorite thing about our house is that my children's friends like to hang out here," Louise says. "The home is well-done, but nothing is too fancy or off-limits. We actually live in every single room; it simply feels like us." CS

Other inspired accents, such as the 17 framed sketches of cathedrals and churches that line the landing wall, personalize the home's décor.

FAMILY COTTAGE

Treasure hunter and decorator Carla Edgeworth's creativity and practicality produced the eclectic style found in this family–friendly home.

This completely updated 1930s cottage was a lucky find by the Edgeworth family. Carla and her husband, Alex, were delighted that the only work necessary was cosmetic. So once the painting was complete, the hunt for unique but practical decorating items began. "Three children under the age of 7 will keep you practical," Carla says, but it hasn't stifled her sense of style here.

The kitchen-family room combination is done in neutrals with washable linen slipcovers and white walls. With the sophisticated touches of dark gray on doors and trims, as well as the far kitchen wall, the room is far from being ho-hum beige. Large, comfy furniture is just right for adults to relax in and for little ones to climb.

(Clockwise from top left) Sleek brass hardware adds a polished sophistication to this contemporary kitchen. Hanging a collection of rolling pins is a creative storage solution that also serves as kitchen décor. This collection is attached to beadboard and framed to hang, resulting in a unique focal point that exudes an effortless cottage style. A rustic antique sconce hangs next to the kitchen window above the sink.

The butler's pantry in the hall provides a second sink and a refrigerator for beverages.

The children's areas received as much design attention as the living areas. In the large playroom, an old wooden feedbox now stores toys. Pull-down maps add color to the white walls. The window treatments were made from old flag pieces and hung with rope. The interesting light fixture was purchased directly from its designer.

(Above) Old flags were sewn into Roman shades for the oldest boy's room, adding a pop of color at the windows. Antique prints hang alongside the bed, and a red monogram announces who sleeps in this bed.

(Left) Alex cut a collection of boards into a unique shape to hang on the guest bathroom wall for textural interest, which highlights the room's crisp white features.

The bedrooms are full of found treasures, including the beds. Avoiding kid-specific themes, Carla designed rooms that will grow with the children. Accessories atop a clean, white base are easy to change as the interests of the kids evolve. The Edgeworth home is full of fabulous finds, and when combined with the clean lines of the décor, they create a treasure of a home for the family. CS

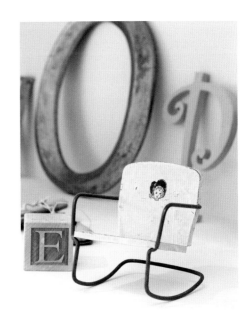

(Clockwise from top left) A baby dress is displayed from an old plate rack. The small letter block was a newborn gift with the baby's initial and birth details. Thrift-store headboards reupholstered in a purple hue set the tone for Amelia's bedroom.

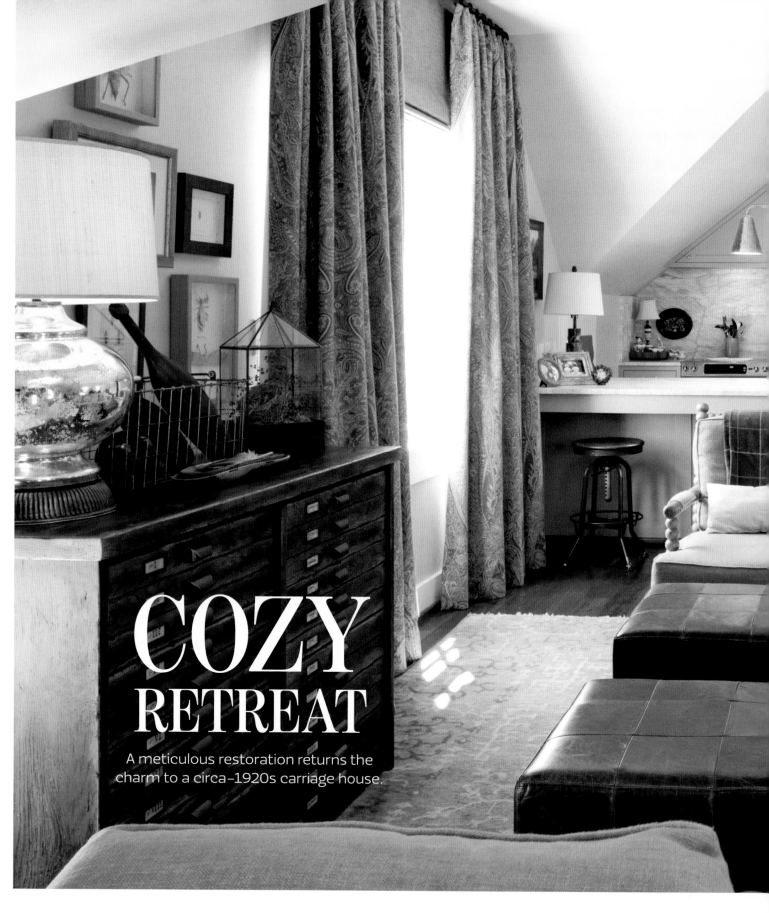

COZY
RETREAT

A meticulous restoration returns the charm to a circa–1920s carriage house.

everal years ago, Vicki and Harrison Brannon decided to restore their venerable stone-covered home's companion carriage house, so Vicki partnered with designer Michaele Travis of Michaele Travis Interior Design, Inc. to bring the redo to life. The collaboration resulted in period-perfect quarters that embody the beauty and character of the property's 1926 roots.

"Every client's needs are different," Michaele says, noting Vicki prefers hands-on participation. "I wanted to look, hunt, and see for myself," Vicki adds with a smile. The two searched high and low for the most authentic materials, like the reclaimed hardwood floors that were made in the 1920s at a nearby mill. They replaced all of the hardware with age-accurate pieces, scoured the inventory at an architectural salvage store for vintage doorknobs, and incorporated cherished family heirlooms. cs

Neutral-hued walls and rich brown accents combine to create a comfortable and serene retreat.

STYLE IDEA If the walls are low and angled you can still hang art. Here art and a cozy corner chair with a reading lamp help make the space feel complete.

BRIGHT
SPOTS

A homeowner uses well-placed
accessories to add pops of
color and visual interest to an
otherwise neutral-hued home.

An all-white design scheme presents a peaceful appearance to be sure, but Linda Johnson's home proves the point that a dash of color can truly bring a space to life. The home's neutral background allows cherished wood furniture, like the antique gateleg table and burled chest in the central room, to capture its proper attention. From vivid orange cookware displayed in the kitchen to bright bouquets of fresh-clipped blooms scattered throughout the house, Linda has created a home that is both relaxing and cheerful. CS

White and Airy

In the master suite, Linda accessorized the bed with vintage linens found in an antiques shop in England's Cotswolds. Shams featuring red turkey stitch bring a sprinkling of color to the sunlit space, as do the blue-and-white ginger jar lamps and floral cushions propped in a pair of wicker chairs. Fresh-cut flowers from Linda's garden add both color and charm.

STYLE INSPIRATIONS

Nothing evokes quintessential cottage charm like a whitewashed picket fence. You can recreate that cottage style with crisp white outdoor furnishings that give a playful nod to times gone by while offering practical form and function to your space.

CHAPTER FIVE

COLLECTIONS AND DISPLAYS

ARTISTIC PASSION

Scientific works of art created by early explorers continue to inspire and influence collectors today.

A rt collector and curator Gilbert Johnston's passion for natural history garners him a deep appreciation for artist John J. Audubon and other natural artists of the 17th, 18th, and 19th centuries. During those times people were immersed in nature—traveling primarily by carriage, horseback, or on foot—and they were curious of their surroundings. It's a lifestyle that's often difficult for people of the 21st century to fully imagine. Gilbert shares that people of that time were willing to pay huge sums of money for bound nature prints to use as a learning tool for the world around them.

Today these prints and reproductions alike are not only a learning tool but an investment, Gilbert says. "You're buying something that's beautiful that you must understand to appreciate," he adds. "When you learn about the courageous people who dedicated their lives to doing this—risking their lives and sometimes their fortunes—you see that it's more than just an image; it's symbolic of the sacrifice of the person who produced it."

Gilbert shares his passion for natural history and art by presenting lectures and selling a wide variety of original antique artwork.

CANEWARE
CHARM

Known for its utility and delicate beauty, caneware remains a sought-after commodity among serious collectors of vintage pottery.

The term caneware was derived from early pieces depicting bound bamboo reeds, wheat, and other stalk-like vegetation. Caneware lacks the colors characteristic of more ornamental ceramics; rather, it's composed of tan smear-glazed or unglazed stoneware that works well as tea sets, tureens, and jugs. Other forms that came into vogue during Josiah Wedgwood's time were game-pie dishes, which often convey hunting and captured fowl motifs, along with stylized rims that resemble the pastry crust of meat pies.

As with most popular things, Wedgwood's pottery was often copied by competing potters, both in England and abroad. Even after his death in 1795, his sons kept the factory running, which continued making caneware well into the 19th century. While these objects were often used for cooking and serving food, many of them have survived to enhance our world with their beauty and delicate artistry.

(Opposite, top) This trio of smear–glazed jugs of graduated size were potted by E. Jones of Cobridge, England, in the heyday of English caneware. (Right) This cheese dome perfectly demonstrates the functional aspects of caneware. Note its livestock and thistle details, along with a flower finial as the finishing touch.

COLLECTING
MEMORIES

Inspired by a love of history, this elegant cottage
is filled with beautiful keepsakes and collections.

his small cottage is a compilation of
a lifetime of treasures collected by the
homeowners on various trips with family
and friends. Plenty of large windows
draw the eye outdoors and allow soft, natural
light to blanket each room, showcasing the
beauty of their precious white collectibles and
cherished antiques. CS

STYLE IDEA With an extensive collection of china, artwork, and other fine keepsakes, the homeowners added a shelf above the windows in the dining room to allow for more space to display beloved items. This idea works well in any room of the house.

A display of white decorative serveware is showcased on a salvaged sideboard and hutch.

NATURE'S GIFTS

As we walk along the shore, shells seem to beckon us to pluck them from the sand. Collecting them is hard to resist, especially since they're a gift from the sea.

STYLE IDEA Turn old shells into a work of art with a high–intensity glue gun. Use a flat frame made of wood or clay. Covering an entire frame will take more shells than you expect, so gather lots of them. The glue sets pretty quickly, which means the finished product will be ready for a photo in no time.

*I*nspired by a shell-covered box he found at an antiques shop, artist Johnny Sims began collecting seashells for a project of his own. From Key Largo to Key West he combed the beaches for treasures. He also orders shells in bulk from wholesalers and even talked a Florida restaurant owner into saving oyster shells for him. From his studio, dubbed the Shell Shack, Johnny creates beautiful picture frames, mirrors, boxes, and even chandeliers decked in gifts from the sea. The soft monochromatic palette of the shells offers a subtle sheen to any space. Johnny's biggest job to date is the pair of 8x4-foot oyster shell mirrors for the casino in the Atlantis Hotel in the Bahamas.

RESOURCES

ARCHITECTS
Page 10, 26–35
Gary L. Brewer
Robert A.M. Stern Architects
ramsa.com

Page 64–69
Ross Chapin
Ross Chapin Architects
rosschapin.com

Page 80–83
Scott Merrill
Merrill, Pastor & Colgan Architects
merrillpastor.com

Page 116–122
Jim Barganier
Barganier Davis Sims Architects
Associated
bdsarch.com

INTERIORS
Page 22–25
Mandi Smith T
Mandi Smith T Interiors
mandismithinteriors.com

Page 36–43
Grace Cribbin
auberginehome.com

Page 52–63
Nikie Barfield
Nikie Barfield Design
nikiebarfield.com

Page 102–107
Pandy Agnew
Pandy Agnew Interiors
thegoodlifebirmingham.com

Page 124–129
Tonya G. Kilpatrick
Kilpatrick Designs
tonyakilpatrick@live.com

Page 130–137
Lynn Myers
Lynn Myers Designs
lynnmyersdesigns.com

Page 138–143
Laurel–Dawn McBurney
abodelove.blogspot.com

Page 148–157
Lisa Flake
Caldwell Flake Interiors
caldwellflake.com

Page 158–167
Carla Edgeworth
CE Tolivers
caedgeworth@bellsouth.net

Page 168–173
Michaele Travis
Michaele Travis Interior Designs Inc.
205–296–8168

BUILDERS
Page 18–21
Imagineered Homes, LLC
imagineeredhomes.com

Page 108–115
Francis A. Bryant & Sons
fabryant.com

SHOPS
Page 12–17
Smith's Antiques Mall
850–654–1484

Antiques on Holiday
850–837–0488

Lola's on 30A
850–660–1662

Page 44–45
Taylor Linens
taylorlinens.com

Page 94–101
White Flowers
whiteflowers.com

Page 144
Tricia's Treasures
triciastreasures.us

Page 144–145
Sew Sheri Designs
sewsheri.com

Page 186–187
Gilbert Johnston
antiquenatureprints.com

Page 188–191
The Brown House: Antiques, Art,
Comforts of Life
thebrownhouse.bigcartel.com

Page 192–197
Sherry Eldridge
Trussville Antiques & Interiors
205–661–9805

ARTISTS
Page 12–17
Sherry Sandquist
palmettocottage@aol.com

Page 84–89
Laura Clark Artistry
lauraclarkartistry.com

Page 198–201
Johnny Sims
205–229–5372

RENTALS
Page 78–83
Sunburst Beach Vacations
sunburstbeachvacations.com